Wiggle Waggle

JONATHAN LONDON

Illustrated by MICHAEL REX

Silver Whistle

Harcourt Brace & Company

San Diego   New York   London

Printed in Singapore

Many animals walk,
and so do you.
Some *walk* funny
or *hop* like a bunny.
Now this is your chance
to do an animal dance!

How does a duck walk?

wiggle waggle,

wiggle waggle.

How does a horse walk?

Clippity-clop, clippity-clop.

How does an
elephant walk?

CLOMP, CLOMP,

CLOMP.

How does
a camel walk?

GAL**UMPH**,

GAL**UMPH**,

GALUMPH.

How does a penguin walk?

Wibble *waddle,*

wibble *waddle.*

How does a pig walk?

Snuffle root,

snuffle root.

How does a frog walk?

FLOP!

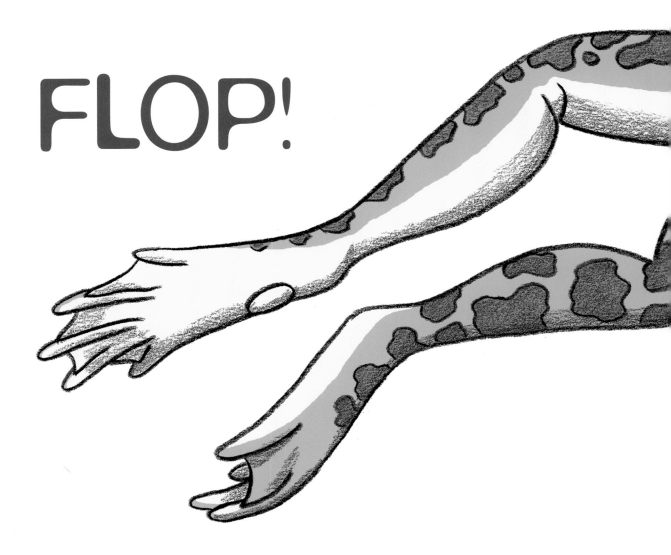

FLOP! FLOP!

How does a bear walk?

BUMBLE *ROLL*,

BUMBLE *ROLL.*

How does a cat walk?

Pish-posh,

pish-posh.

How does a kangaroo walk?

BOING!
BOING!

BOING!

Now all together—
Let's wiggle a feather!

**Wiggle waggle,
wiggle waggle,**
goes the duck.

*Clippity-clop,
clippity-clop,*
goes the horse.

CLOMP,
CLOMP,
CLOMP,
goes the elephant.

GALUMPH, GALUMPH, GALUMPH,
goes the camel.

Wibble *waddle*,
  wibble *waddle*,
goes the penguin.

Snuffle root, snuffle root,
goes the pig.

FLOP! **FLOP!** FLOP!
goes the frog.

BUMBLE *ROLL*, **BUMBLE** *ROLL*, goes the bear.

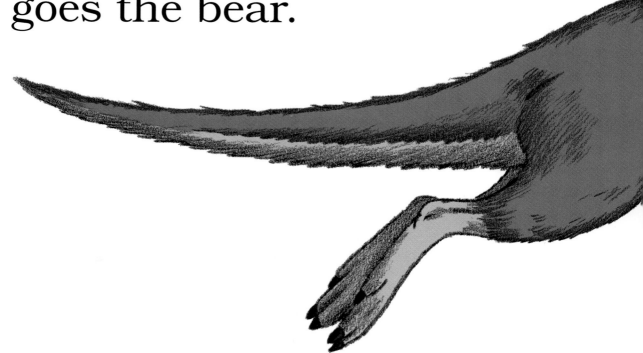

Pish-posh,
pish-posh,
goes the cat.

BOING! BOING! BOING!
goes the kangaroo.

And now we're through.

What about you?

For Claire and Marc, who can walk like a duck
— J. L.

For Kelsey, who walks with me
— M. R.

Library of Congress Cataloging-in-Publication Data
London, Jonathan, 1947–
Wiggle waggle/by Jonathan London; illustrated by Michael Rex.
p.   cm.
"Silver Whistle."
Summary: Describes how various animals walk, from the
wiggle waggle of a duck to the boing, boing, boing of a kangaroo.
ISBN 0-15-201940-5
[1. Animal locomotion—Fiction.   2. Animals—Fiction.]
I. Rex, Michael, ill.   II. Title.
PZ7.L8432Wj   1999
[E]—dc21   98-10773

G   I   K   M   N   L   J   H

The illustrations in this book were done in colored pencil.
The coloring was done with Adobe® Graphic Software.
The display type was set in Elroy.
The text type was set in Bookman.
Color separations by Bright Arts Graphics Pte. Ltd., Singapore
Printed and bound by Tien Wah Press, Singapore
Production supervision by Stanley Redfern
Designed by Lydia D'moch